Contents

The Alpha Male: MAN UP and Unlock Your Alpha

An Overnight Guide to Conquering Fear, Women, and Lifelong Success

By C.K. Murray

Similar works by C.K. Murray:

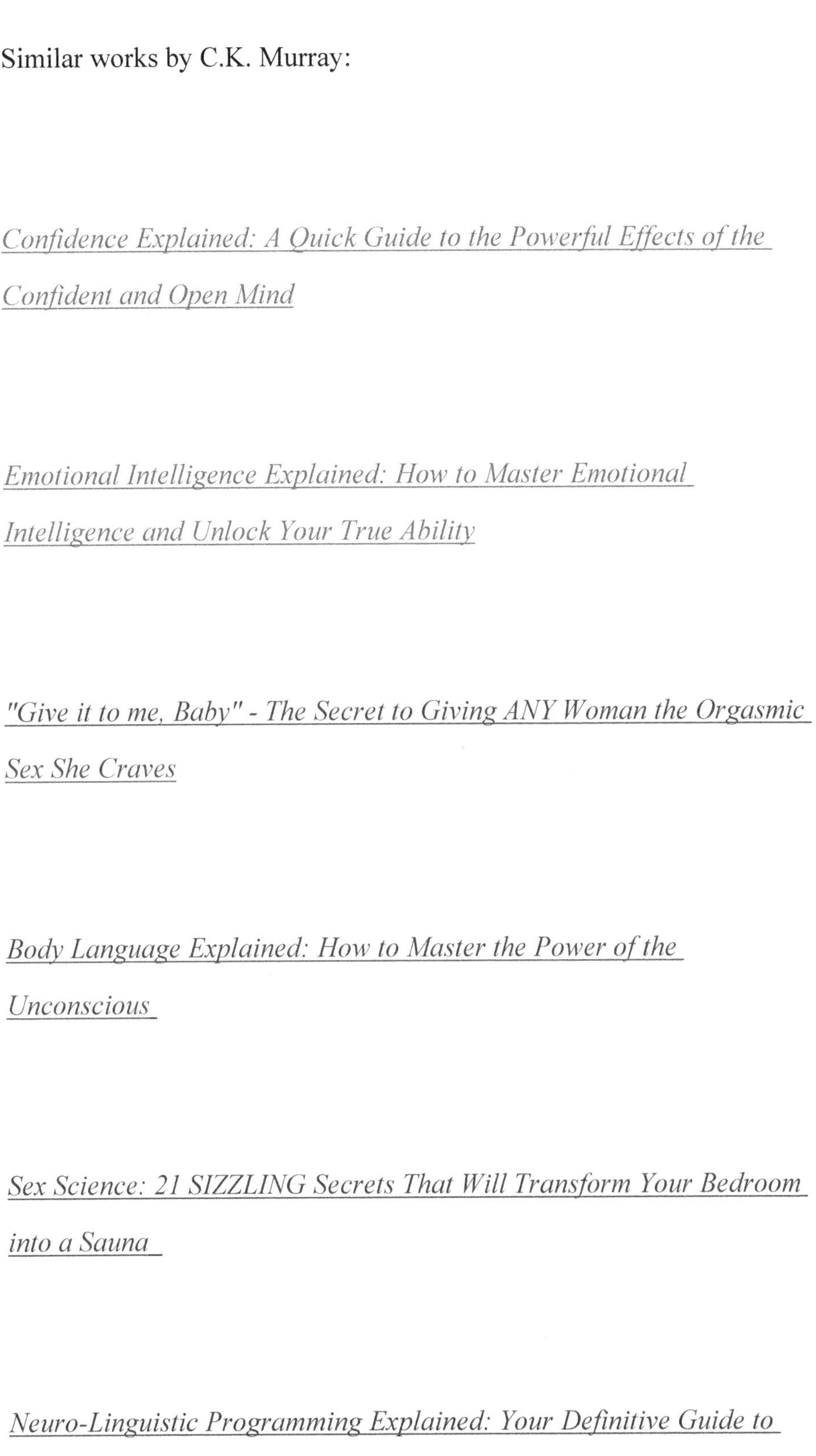

Confidence Explained: A Quick Guide to the Powerful Effects of the Confident and Open Mind

Emotional Intelligence Explained: How to Master Emotional Intelligence and Unlock Your True Ability

"Give it to me, Baby" - The Secret to Giving ANY Woman the Orgasmic Sex She Craves

Body Language Explained: How to Master the Power of the Unconscious

Sex Science: 21 SIZZLING Secrets That Will Transform Your Bedroom into a Sauna

Neuro-Linguistic Programming Explained: Your Definitive Guide to

"The mass of men lead lives of quiet desperation"

~ Henry David Thoreau

Before you do anything else... Stop.

Good, now let go. Let go of your bullshit, your excuses, your reasons for being weak. For being *beta*.

Look yourself in the mirror, and admit it. You've failed.

You don't look hearing it and you sure as hell don't like thinking it. But it's true. You know it, and I know it.

The reason you're reading this book is because you've failed. You're not where you could be, or *should* be. And it's entirely your fault.

You've failed because you've feared. You've allowed this fear to infiltrate every corner and crevice of your life. You've permitted your insecurities to reign supreme. Sometimes they take the form of anxiety, sometimes despair or dejection, and many times, more times than you can count, a quiet desperation.

Instead of seizing each and every day, you've lost your grasp. You get up in the morning tired and uncertain, convinced that your life is going to continue more or less the same. Maybe you're just floating along, barely treading water. Or maybe you've had *some* success, but not nearly enough to make it all worth it.

No matter where you are, no matter *who* you are, no matter *what* you are—you're capable of so much more, if you go for it.

So let's get it…

Ch. 1 - The Alpha is Inside ALL of Us

Every man wants to be an alpha male, the kind of real man that gets what he wants when he wants it. There is nobody alive who wants to slink through life weak and broken like some sad-sack without a future. Nobody wants to be just another average Joe.

So then why do so many guys blow it?

If you want to unleash your alpha overnight, you need to know what you want. Before you can become it, you must envision it. And when it comes to envisioning the alpha male, nothing says dominance like a powerful man.

Alpha Males are different. They're a different breed, a different mold. They walk into any room, any situation, any context—no matter the con*tent*—and they dominate. Women's heads turn, their feet point, their hearts flutter. The alpha male knows that all eyes are on him and he doesn't even flinch. In fact, he *embraces* it.

Alpha men are undeniable. Their presence, unmistakable. They walk taller, speak smoother, think faster and act quicker than all around them. Men either hate them or revere them. Women crave them. Their auras are commanding, their communication skills untouchable. But none of this—none of these expectations—are burdensome.

For the Alpha Male it's just business as usual.

For the Alpha Male, confidence is never in short supply. Size doesn't matter. Height or weight doesn't matter. Alpha Men could care less if they look like Brad Pitt or an *olive* pit.

Why?

Because fuck insecurity, that's why. The Alpha Male gets results and he knows it.

From Wimp to Winner

If you want to stop soiling your pants at the thought of beautiful women, if you're tired of suffering under your bosses' demands, tired of being somebody *else*'s bitch, feeling like Life's bitch—then it's time to MAN UP.

For the Alpha Male, there is no such thing as failure. *Failing* is one thing—but fail*ure* denotes finality. It signals that the outcome is set in stone and nothing can be done. This is horseshit. Alpha Males don't call their friends sulking because they've messed up. They don't get sad and pissy because somebody else outdid them, outperformed them, or beat them to the punch. Alpha Males don't mope around getting drunk because "life isn't fair." Alpha Males wakeup, own up, and know that one failure is the gateway to multiple successes. Even multiple failures do not mean that things are done.

Alpha Males go where others do not.

This is why Alpha Males see failing as no more than a stepping stone. They are natural trend-setters. They carve their own niche. They have the balls to go where wimps wouldn't dare. Other people worry about social expectations; Alpha Males create those expectations. They forge powerfully ahead to the sound of their own drummer, undeterred by what is 'normal' or 'standard.'

The reason the Alpha Male doesn't worry is because he's comfortable with who he is. See, the problem with most men is their insecurity. They want to look one way on the outside, but half the time they don't even believe it. They spend too much time creating some fragile image that shatters at Life's major twists and turns. This persona of theirs is created to appease everybody else, because the average man wants nothing more than to be accepted.

The Alpha Male, however, just keeps on going. No doubts, no excuses.

Everybody has a reason for being average. The Alpha Male doesn't *understand* average.

The reason that the Alpha Male doesn't comprehend mediocrity is because mediocrity is the result of weakness. It's what most men settle for. By and large, weak men internalize a perception of themselves, and never change. They never push, they never fight. They lack the passion and the drive to go after what they really want. They are weak of mind and more often than not, weak of body. If things don't go their way after a while, they stop pushing and settle.

The Alpha Male never settles. He is filled with passion, a fire that mesmerizes women, captivates peers, and recreates reality.

Have you ever been in a room and practically *felt* the charge of somebody else?

This is not figurative. Alpha Males actually give off a more palpable energy than most people. We all have electricity pulsing through us, this is a fact. This energy is a lifeblood, our vitality. It is the reason that some people are said to have an 'electric' personality. An 'aura' or power.

Alpha Males are aware of that power. They know that the way they portray themselves, carry themselves, move and maneuver themselves—is all part of defining that power. More than anything, they are intent on growing that power. They use that power to create the life they dream of, and nobody—*nobody*—can prevent them from that goal.

Many people are complacent. The Alpha Male is never complacent. You think Warren Buffet, or Bill Gates, or Steve Jobs reached their heights by accepting that their dreams were unrealistic? Do you think they listened when critics told them early on to "get a real job"?

The Alpha Male is not just another fish in the sea.

The reason the Alpha Male is able to navigate his own path is because of his head. The Alpha Male isn't always the smartest person in the room, but he knows what to *do* with his smarts. Applying this intelligence means that the Alpha Male has a comprehensive advantage. He can master his emotions and master his rational thinking. He is not an emotional creature. The Alpha Male is cool-headed and calculating, capable of resisting weak emotions and conquering emotional intelligence. He is a man of composure, and does not succumb to moments of weakness like all the other *boys* masquerading as men.

Other men pretend to be something they're not. The Alpha Male is what he is, and doesn't stray. He has fashioned himself, physically, mentally, emotionally—in a way that is honest. He doesn't betray his morals or step on his values because of others. He refuses, outright, to abandon his principles when times get tough. The Alpha Male is a man of high morals and will stick to those morals no matter what. This is what other men seem to struggle with. They don't know what they believe, their core values are flimsy and may shift on a whim. The reason their values change is because they don't have a firm foundation.

And the reason most men don't have a firm foundation is because they don't know who they are.

For the Alpha Male, identity is everything. He knows that the most important thing in life is finding what makes him tick; what makes life truly worth living. This is why the Alpha Male is always primed for success. He doesn't follow the lead of others down some predetermined path. He follows his own lead, leading by example, through his mannerisms, his language, his words and wisdom. Alpha Males know who they are and don't succumb to their egos. While some men may put on a tough front, they are often weak on the inside. The Alpha Male, by comparison, has no falsehood. He is his own man, without pretense— one of the main reasons women love him.

The Alpha Male is not always born. He is often made through years of steady, singular focus. He is created through his perceptions and his plays, day by day, move by measured move. When an Alpha Male looks at his goals, his visions, his desires—and he has many—he *knows*. The Alpha Male knows that everything is a process.

Only fools think otherwise. Only *fools* assert to know everything, to have their lives in perfect, absolute order.

The Alpha Male is constantly growing and constantly refining and pursuing his purpose. His priorities may change, his outcomes may differ, but at the end of the day he is always the same in one, fundamental way:

His appetite for growth is insatiable.

Personal development is the quality most integral to the Alpha Male. Without it, nobody can go anywhere. The Alpha Male knows this first and foremost, and he doesn't worry when immediate success eludes him. Self-improvement is a journey, a process. He is a powerful person because his power is derived from this process. His focus on this process is unflinching.

Because the process is so important to the Alpha Male, he enlists the help of others. He knows that though he is a leader, there is always something to be learned from others. He is well-mannered, allowing peers and even subordinates to share their ideas and opinions. He does not strive to 'one-up' anybody because doing so is only proof of insecurity. This is why the Alpha Male is so successful. He is clever and cunning, using a special mind that delivers special functions. He is able to quickly assess situations, strengths, weaknesses, obstacles and opportunities. While he does not always voice his understanding, he shows it in other, more subtle ways. His analytical mind ensures that no situation—no matter how emotionally tinged—is outside his realm of reason.

His levelheaded approach to complex situations allows him to deal with things much easier than most people. He is even levelheaded in the face of his own faults and errors. He will admit when he is wrong and hold himself accountable. Weaker men will scurry away or hide from the truth, but the Alpha Male has nowhere to run. Instead of withering in the shadows, the Alpha Male is secure in the light. He will bring his mistakes to light and apologize to anybody who is affected. Again, his focus on the process means that he sees these personal blunders as nothing less than opportunities for growth.

His passion will not be weakened.

But passion should not be confused with aggression. Too many times, guys try to be Alpha Males by acting tough and looking tougher. They hit the gym, they sculpt their bodies and look for fights, preying on any *betas* that come their way. They think that flexing their muscles and hounding women is going to make them threatening and alpha.

It doesn't. It makes them *fools*.

This isn't the animal kingdom. Those who are confident don't have to flaunt it. You think Bruce Lee walked into a room and made it known to *everybody* that he could kick their ass? Of course not. He didn't have to, because it was known. Alpha men don't have to roar to be heard. Others can sense it, they can feel it, they can see it emanating off the Alpha.

Only weak men feel compelled to use aggression as a means of *faking* alpha status. The Alpha Male doesn't flaunt it. He lives it.

Another reason the Alpha Male is so powerful is because he knows who to hang with. Truth be told, you are your surroundings. The fusion of nature and nurture means that our environments play a large role in shaping us. If you surround yourself with weaklings and losers, you're going to slowly but surely adopt their attitudes and behaviors.

The Alpha Male surrounds himself with winners. His friends are intelligent, his coworkers are motivated, his women beautiful, his family fiercely caring. He is a man that knows that there is strength in numbers. He learns from those whose talents are varied, and embraces the words and wisdom of those more successful. While beta men pretend to be perfect, the Alpha Male admits his flaws. It is only through coming to grips with one's shortcomings, that those shortcomings are overcome.

But again, most men are weak. They don't know how to change their lives in a way that is beneficial. Instead they slink through the world feeling sorry for themselves, hating on those with more success, and spending their down-time fantasizing of greatness.

Real men go after success. And if you want to be a real man, an Alpha Man, you need to know how to get there. All this talk so far is great, but it's just talk. It's just talk until you go out and make it more than just talk. So walk the walk, learn what you need and what you don't.

The time is now...

Ch. 2 - F*ck Fear. It's Time to Man Up

The reason you're not an alpha male *today* is because you're not fearless.

It's a simple truth, but one that is nearly impossible for most men to overcome. More often than not, weak men do and say the wrong things, again and again. The reason this happens is because most men are afraid. They over analyze, they over-internalize, and then they doubt. They let their emotions take control and tinge their thinking. Instead of proceeding with a keen rational mind, their insecurities creep in and fuck it all up.

When they aren't being scared little vermin, beta males try acting like something they're not. Unfortunately, this rarely works. Most women can pick up on fake guys, just like most guys can pick up on fake breasts!

Phony men are real embarrassing. Anybody with half a mind can see through them. You've probably seen these types of guys out and about, acting like fools to impress women. They act tough around guys, brag about their victories, exaggerate their accomplishments, and generally come across as desperate, clueless fools.

They're not amusing and they're not impressive. They're *weak*.

The problem with weak men is how incapable they are. Weak men could be spending every day, every moment, becoming stronger, more secure men. But they don't. They become complacent. The consider things "good enough," convinced that sitting back on their laurels is going to make everything hunky-dory.

What beta men have to understand is that their weakness can be fixed. As much as they have yet to learn about being an *alpha*, they have just as much to learn about *not* being a beta.

Top Mistakes ALL Men Must Avoid

Beta males are barely males.

They possess traits that make them more women than men. They are emotional creatures, often hiding these pathetic soft spots through a variety of defense mechanisms. They may adopt authoritarian mindsets, they may be overly angry, they may workout excessively, they may drink or drug excessively, and they may retreat into the deep, dark depths of depression.

More often times than not, they're whiny, complaining, and externally-based. All reasons for their struggles are external. The world is against them and there's no way that somebody like them could ever truly succeed. Alpha Males make them jealous and spiteful. Beautiful women make them angry yet scared. In general, more successful people leave the beta male dejected.

Beta males want the world to change around them, because they don't have the balls to work for their own success. They're too scared because they believe that failure is more likely. They believe that others will get in their way, and this prospect frightens them. Beta males do not know how to deal with conflict. They either overreact, allowing emotion to make them look like fools, or they run away, avoiding conflict at all costs. They have no conception of a balanced approach to conflict, one in which reason and understanding replace emotional breakdown.

This is why beta males rarely move beyond their comfort zones. They keep things familiar and safe—anything outside of their little bubbles is deemed too threatening. Because of this, beta males fail to grow. When Life comes with a little bite, beta males retreat. Instead of challenging themselves and becoming men, they fall back on their bums like kids in a sandlot.

If you think you're slipping into beta male habits, it's time to look closer. Consider the telltale signs.

See, most beta men are *risk-averse*. If you're risk averse, it means that you don't like to go after things. You'd rather let others dictate your life because you don't believe you can make it happen. You rarely branch outside your comfort zone and rarely *think* about going outside it. Chances are, you've been in the same job or career for a long time, doing the same things. You're not adventurous so you don't travel the world or take new risks, and you're not courageous, so you fear anything that can lead to mistakes. For these reasons, other people— especially women—think that you're boring and unmotivated.

Beta males never achieve their dreams, though they always have a reason why. They never take their own lead, yet they always have a reason why. They don't like to ruffle feathers and they don't like to speak their mind, which is why they hardly exist. Their personalities are flimsy if not fake. They do their best to fade into the background and fit in, which is why they are so weak. They're bad at making decisions, they're bad at making suggestions, and they're even worse at taking them.

Beta males are victims to their egos. Because they can never balance their pride and insecurity, they don't know what to do. They quietly follow in others' paths, even when they may outright deny doing so. They're too insecure to admit when they need to follow others, and too insecure to ever start off own their own path. Instead they exist somewhere in the middle, convincing themselves of their 'uniqueness' when in reality they do nothing different from all the other nobodies.

Because beta males do not have a formal identity, they seek the words of others. Beta men *depend* upon positive affirmation and reinforcement from peers, friends, family and coworkers. Their need for approval can reach almost pathological levels. They become so needy, so painfully desperate for affection and love, that the slightest period of neglect can destroy them.

When seeking the approval of others, the beta male is often unsure. He will ask questions such as "Did I do good?" or "Was that okay?" in order to assess his performance. He can't stand the thought of being disliked, and will do anything to correct his behavior to appease others.

The beta male is quite timid at times, asking for permission when it is not required, and become really antsy when approached by others. The beta male is so bent on appealing to these 'others,' that he will rarely say "no." Even if agreeing to something puts the beta male in conflict with his morals, he will still say "yes." This is because winning the approval of others is more important to the beta male than his own values. Of course, more often than not the beta male doesn't *have* any consistent values.

When a social interaction goes wrong, the beta male will overcompensate by trying too hard to be funny or entertaining. He will become something he is not in hopes that it is what the others are looking for. After social interactions gone wrong, the beta male will spend a lot of alone time doubting and berating himself for his mess up. In many cases the beta male will think the interaction went poorly even if it didn't. Again, this is all a result of the beta male's low self-esteem.

The self-esteem of a beta male is devastating. Because he lacks confidence, he will engage in a variety of thought patterns that are negative. He expects things to go *okay* at best, and will easily become defensive or critical if accused of wrongdoing. Of course, the reason for his wrongdoing is his attitude. He just can't seem to see beyond the negatives, even when the positives are right in front of his face. He is negative about his job prospects, negative about his current interpersonal relations, negative about his chances with women, negative about his past, negative about his future, and almost always negative about his body image.

Because of all this negativity, it is no surprise that many beta males suffer from social phobia and shyness. In order to hide this, they may become distinctly anti-social, lashing out and authority figures and defying laws in order to gain attention and seem 'bad.'

In the end, as too many beta males find out, nothing *good* comes from being 'bad.' Unless, of course, your goal is to attract insecure women...

Key Strategies for Transforming Your Self-Confidence

So what do you think?

Do you see where you've been going wrong? Can you understand how your attitudes and behaviors *significantly* affect your daily life?

If you still struggle with transforming yourself from a beta male to an alpha male, the hardest part is gaining self-esteem. Self-confidence is the stepping stone to everything else. Without a secure and powerful foundation, your other efforts aren't going to mean jack squat. You have to be assured in your ability before you take that first step. Otherwise, you're stepping off a cliff.

In order to supercharge your self-esteem, all you need to do is change your thoughts. This may sound difficult but it's easy if you allow it to happen. Don't fight the positivity you so desperately need. Allow positive thoughts to flow through your head, even if you don't initially believe them.

Here's how:

Remember what you're good at

And please, don't start by saying "I'm not good at anything." Based purely on statistics there is always going to be somebody better and worse than you, so don't be mad if you consider yourself no more than average. Instead of thinking how poorly you do in one area compared to others, think about how well you do compared to the others below you.

Remind yourself how people with less than you are motivated.

And think why.

If these people are motivated, then surely you have no excuses not to be? So remember your strengths. Write them down, categorize them, create a numerical ranking that changes over time as you work on them. Whatever you wanna do, make sure that you do in visual format. The key is to have your strengths up there in your face. Continue to foster these abilities that you believe are your best, but don't let them get in the way of cultivating your weaknesses. Note your weaknesses in smaller text, maybe with an asterisk. Make them visible but not the prominent thing that you see. You do this for one reason and one reason only: You draw upon your strengths to improve your weaknesses. If your weaknesses are center-stage, you'll only think about them and ignore your strengths. But if you don't list your weaknesses at all, you'll end up becoming complacent.

Self-Efficacy

As one of the fathers of social psychology, Albert Bandura, has discovered, believing in yourself can go a *looong* way. When Bandura developed the term self-efficacy, he was referring to an individual's self-appraisal of task completion. In other words, a person with high self-efficacy more readily believes in his or her ability to 'get it done.' A person with low self-efficacy doesn't believe it. For these reasons, the more often you meet with success, the more likely you are to try. If you constantly fail, you'll try less and believe less.

In order to boost self-efficacy, you need only look at your successes.

You should strive to build on small, realistic, measurable goals that allow room for long-term growth. You should also learn to embrace positivity from multiple sources. Listen to peers, family members, the media—any source that provides positivity.

The trick is to be selective. All of these sources can provide negativity too, so it's up to you to guide them in a more positive direction. Watch only television shows that gear you up for your own dreams. Ask your friends, peers and family members how they approached their own successes and how they overcame their obstacles.

Self-efficacy may hinge on self-appraisal, but it can certainly be strengthened by those around you.

Find Your Template

It's time to find your template. Find somebody who is great and successful. Find the right crowd. Hang with relatives who have paved their way. Hang with other powerful men and their friends. Hang with people who surround themselves with beautiful, successful people— and women!

Most importantly, find somebody who is honest. Make sure that they're honest and optimistic. If they're honest but have a terrible attitude, you're not going to feel good (even if they do give you the truth). If you admire the person, model the person. Connecting and learning is all-too-important, and if you find that rare person that affords you a real connection—you're golden.

Self-talk

Beta males tell themselves, "I can't do this" or "I'm not good at that." They'll overuse contractions and focus on absolutes such as "always" or "never" or "ever."

Eliminate these words from your vocabulary. The more you say them, whether externally or inside your head, the more you believe them. So think about that. Consider the importance of giving everything you have when you talk to yourself.

Talk to yourself in positive realistic words. You don't have to be feeding yourself bullshit, but you sure as hell have to be feeding yourself something. And if you're going to feed yourself something, why feed it poison? Why tell yourself that you're no good or that things won't change?

Does that work for you? Does that make you wake up in the morning feeling motivated? Does it gear you up for achieving success?

Of course not!

So stop with the negative self-talk. After a while it becomes a record that you unconsciously adopt. And then you're screwed.

Create a comfort space

You don't have to own villas in the Caribbean or homes across the world. You don't even have to live in a nice place to begin with. What matters is that you give your place, your space, a flavor of who you are. Don't surround yourself with dim walls and crummy decorations.

Create a place that reflects your self-image. The point is to be confident in who you are and create a space that echoes that confidence. This means creating an environment that is motivating and attractive. A place that is clean, comfortable and aesthetically pleasing. This will charge you up for success.

If your place is a rat's nest where you cant find anything, you're going to end up failing more often than not. This is because your living space represents your inner space. If you change your living space, you change how you perceive your more personal environment—your insides. A clean well-furnished room with motivating posters, portraits and the like is more likely to keep you positive than a dark, dingy place filled with old food and drinks.

Optimism

Tired of hearing this one?

Too bad, it's the only answer to your problems. The reason you don't do as well as you could is because you're too pessimistic. You call it being realistic, but it's not.

Being realistic is believing that you can cultivate an attitude with the right tools. Being unrealistic is believing that you can't cultivate that attitude no matter what you do.

Why would anybody think this?

It's silly to think that bad things are going to happen to you at every turn. That's stupid. What's also stupid is thinking that life is going to hand you roses.

You need to learn to go after your dreams and stop thinking that they're impractical. The only people who tell you they're impractical are the people who failed at theirs. These people likely failed because they were too weak to get what they wanted. Misery likes company, and if you let sad-sacks tell you how to live your life, you're as good as *them*.

And why the heck would you ever want that??

Ch. 3 - SIGNAL Success to ACHIEVE Success – Your Body Language is Your Gateway

Ever heard of body language?

If you haven't, you're living in a nuclear bunker somewhere. If you have, then you know how important it is.

Put simply, body language is everything. And if you can learn how to master the power of the unconscious, you're as good as dominant.

But for those of you who are uninformed, there are several things to remember. Firstly, know that your mind and body are connected. How you appear is how others will perceive you. If you have a beard and unkempt hair with ragged clothes, they'll think you're a hobo or a hippie. If you dress nicely, are clean shaven, and wear a decent suit, they'll think your doing well (even if you're in debt up to your eyeballs!)

But body language is more than just looking clean-cut. Take, for instance, two men. One has a nice thick mane of black hair that is well-kept and trimmed. He is tall and handsome and he wears clothes that fit him well and look good.

The other guy is the same exact thing, down to the same shoes. The only difference? Well, this second guy *carries* himself differently. His chin is held higher, his shoulders back, his eyes ahead.

This guy, dear reader, is showing confident body language. He is signaling through his movements, gestures, expressions and positions that he is confident. Even if he feels insecure at first, merely making these changes will change his mind. Simply standing taller and walking straighter have been shown to increase levels of testosterone while reducing levels of the stress hormone, cortisol.

When a man displays confident body language, other men are more likely to look up to him, and women are more likely to want him. People, in general, will view him as more capable, more strong, more intelligent, and better at the game of Life.

Fair or not, this is how it works.

So if you wanna become an Alpha Male, you have to do it the right way. To achieve success, one must signal success.

Begin signaling success by paying close attention to the signals you are sending. Observe your body language in the mirror or passing by windows or other reflective surfaces.

Firstly, know what *not* to do.

Beta males don't pay attention to the way they move. They walk quickly, nervously, often making jerky motions when deciding where they are going. It is obvious to anybody watching, that the beta male is indecisive. He will swivel from one person to the next, often jerking his body when a new person enters the setting. The beta male is often frenetic when in large social settings, making it painfully apparent that he lacks the confidence to be himself.

When it comes to signals, the only signal the beta male sends is that he is weak and submissive. Many men are unaware that they are displaying body language more fitting of women than men. These clueless males will keep their shoulders slumped with their eyesight usually set below eye-level. They tend to dip their chin when they walk and look down more than around. When uncomfortable in the slightest, they immediately signal this by crossing their arms. Their posture may be stiff and their necks may be craned; they are nervous, anxious and endlessly needy.

When they become too uncomfortable, they retreat. These men will always find excuses for why they have to leave a social setting. And sometimes, they may simply disappear—awkwardly and abruptly.

The reason beta males act like this is because they are constantly in a state of doubt. They're not sure how to end or begin interactions. And because they don't have the wherewithal to initiate, they often wait too late before adopting the proper social cues.

Social situations—no matter how small—can be difficult. For beta males, being in such situations is similar to being exposed. They feel like they're constantly being judged, even though the one doing most the judging is themselves!

In order to combat these feelings, beta males rely on external objects to *defuse* their tension.

This occurs in multiple ways. Firstly, many men will fidget with clothing when nervous. They'll fiddle with their shirt, collar, cuffs, pants or shoes. They may find a nearby object such as a chair or stool and play oddly with it, or move it about with their feet. In worse cases, beta males will sit on their hands, finding a way to hide them. Beta males may also bite their fingers, twiddle their thumbs, or make erratic motions such as tapping, shaking or bouncing.

Their anxiety will also manifest in defensive postures. In these cases, men will position an object between themselves and others. They may hold objects in front of them, oftentimes using their phones as a means of separation. When guarded, beta males will shift their weight away from other people, and many men will even unconsciously cover their genitals, perhaps with their legs closed tight or their hands hanging down. This signals a guarded insecurity, especially around women.

Beta men also indicate their lack of self-esteem through rapid-fire movements. They will often perch on the edge of a chair, facing the nearest exit and seeming like they're going to take off at the slightest threat. They will blink too much during conversations, especially when giving or receiving confidential information. In many cases their eyes will divert or never make contact at all. Many times, the beta male will touch his face in order to unconsciously hide or obscure the truth. This may also occur because the beta male feels like he needs to 'protect' himself from something. Other nervous twitches may include licking his lips, twitching his nose, scrunching his face, and even smiling excessively. Excessive smiling says nothing more than: I aim to please… *everybody*.

Unlike the weak, insecure beta male, the Alpha Male does not aim to please. He knows that others will see him for who he is. He doesn't care if they don't like what they see, because he is confident. And much of the confidence comes from the Alpha male's body language.

When Alpha males enter a room, they do so slowly. They are not rushed or nervous, they do not move from place to place, spot to spot, looking to approach everybody. Instead, they expect others to come to them. When standing in a circle of people, they are usually positioned near the center, with their body language open so as to communicate with all speakers. It is others who angle their bodies to face the Alpha Male, not the other way around.

Because the Alpha Male recognizes his importance, he talks slowly and deliberately. He does not talk for the sake of talking, but reserves comment until there is something worthy to add. Others may bluster and blabber merely to fill the silence. The Alpha Male, however, has no qualms about silence. He is most secure around those who respect his quiet thought.

Unlike nervous thinkers who spout out their ideas or hurriedly work through their thoughts, the Alpha Male is silently but fiercely intelligent. Because he takes the time to think through things and reflect, he never worries about running out of time. When it comes to important meetings and appointments, he usually arrives early to ensure that his strategy is well-planned. He is disciplined but not obsessive. He knows when to unwind and when to work hard.

When working hard, the Alpha Male conveys easy body language. He is always relaxed because he keeps his posture open. His chin is held high and his legs and chest open. He sits with his arms out to the side.

He walks with his shoulders back and his chest and butt out.

When talking to somebody one on one, an Alpha Male will give his full attention, with his head turned fully in your direction and his eyes focused on you. This is because he knows that you value his attention and focus, and will show you that he values your in return.

In short, the Alpha Male is the master of body language. He will mirror facial expressions to show agreement. He will shake with a firm hand and use those hands to accentuate his spoken word. He speaks deliberately with dramatic pauses; his words are carefully considered and expressed.

When establishing a connection, the Alpha Male makes sure to remove barriers in the environment. He smiles like a man that knows what he wants and makes sure to make that smile authentic. When smiling, the Alpha Male ensures that it comes on slowly, lighting up the face and crinkling the eyes. Inauthentic smiles, by comparison, do not crinkle the eyes.

When speaking, the Alpha Male voice is authoritative and consistent, not changing in weird inflections or pitches. Alpha Males will employ a steady voice and a hips-width stance when standing and talking. They will show their palms (a sign of honesty) and tell it like it is.

Of course, it doesn't matter what *it* is, if you don't have the other 'it.'

The other *it,* of course, is the final part of the equation. On one hand is the ability to use powerful body language to your advantage. On the other hand is the ability to use a powerful body, *period.* After all, what's good body language without a good body?

Ch. 4 – But What's Good Body Language Without a Good Body? You Gotta SHAPE UP to MAN UP

Guys with good bodies get good results.

In today's world, the physical is your gateway. If you look like a fat slob, people are going to think you're incapable. They'll stereotype you as some sort of sloth, a man that is too big for his own good. They'll see you as a heart attack waiting to happen. Companies may not want to take a risk on you. After all, why should they invest in you if you haven't invested in yourself?

Why should they risk it if you're in bad shape?

And even if you aren't morbidly obese, being a little bit unfit is going to hurt you. It will hurt your dating prospects, hurt your job prospects, and generally hurt others' perceptions of you.

The problem is, many men don't do what they can to be the healthiest they can.

Truth be told, it doesn't matter what you look like. The vast majority of us don't look like a movie star and we sure as hell don't have the physique of a professional athlete. For these reasons, a lot of us feel like it doesn't really matter. We accept that our genetics aren't ideal and we throw in the towel.

But why?

Why do so many beta males continue to make excuses for why they can't work out? Is it because they're afraid to be seen in a gym? Do they fear the pain of working out, the long-term commitment? Do they tell themselves that they're too tired after a day of work, or that they don't have time?

Or are they just being plain old lazy?

The answer is: all of the above.

See, beta males always have a 'reason' for why they can't workout. They get into a routine of neglecting their bodies, their minds feel crappy as a result, making their bodies feel crappier as a result, which makes their minds feel crappier—and the vicious cycle continues.

Because most guys struggle with getting started, they should start small. If you think you're out-of-shape and have a bad body-image problem, take baby steps. First, find recreational sport leagues with others like you who like a little bit of exercise with a lot of socializing. Purchase a pullup bar and some dumbbells. Start doing pushups and crunches, lift weights around your house, go for runs where nobody can see your out-of-shape body slogging and sweating.

The point is to continue progressing.

Nowadays there are all kinds of gadgets and watches that can track your progress. Heck, feel free to share your metrics with Facebook and

Twitter if you want! Become an exercise nerd. What matters is that you chart your progress, see your improvements, and feel good about it.

Too many people are negative about exercise. They don't seem to realize that exercise is a *necessary* part of healthy living. They don't seem to get that exercise will actually make them feel better. The human body is meant to move, not collect cobwebs.

But this doesn't mean you have to tear down your body with every workout. You don't have to red-line every time you exercise. Simply getting your heart rate up consistently is good to start. After a while, it becomes significantly easier.

When we exercise, our excuses disappear. Do you complain that you're too tired all the time to exercise? Well guess what, sleepyhead... the more you exercise, the more endurance and energy your body and mind have.

People think that routine exercise will wear them out even more. This is false! Routine, moderate exercise will increase your vitality, improve your mood, and generally boost your physical and mental health. You'll also start to embrace other healthy things like eating.

And speaking of eating…

If you don't eat well, you won't feel well. Not to mention you'll be carrying around some extra baggage that can't be good for you (unless your mission is to be a human cushion).

So eat well!

Yea, yeah, yea, you've heard this one a million times before. Chances are you don't know where to start, or—like exercising—lack the motivation. Well, here's a little motivation for ya. You can eat well by eating clean foods. You can also eat clean foods and stay healthy. Oh, and you can eat clean and healthy, *and* do it cheap.

So what's your excuse now?

Do we really need to go into details about this one?--I think not.

Look up a million studies about how clean eating can enhance your performance, your well-being—the whole nine yards. You'll be surprised.

Listen, it's not hard. I know you probably think it requires some dramatic shift in your life, but it doesn't. More likely than not, you know your bad habits. You know if you drink too much soda, eat too much ice cream or pack on too many beer calories. Eating clean is about eating in balance. Some vegetables and fruit and some dairy and some meat. Don't try to eat anything by itself. Eat a mix every-time you eat. Instead of snacking on Oreos, eat some bread with hummus. Or a banana. Instead of guzzling caffeinated coffee, opt for green tea. Substitute fruit infusions for sugary beverages.

Just be smart. Choose the simple, healthy alternative and don't stress it. Think less about the things you're missing and focus on all the things you're getting. And if you find yourself craving those sugary sweets or delicious late night meals, remind yourself of the truth. You're not missing anything. Seriously, you aren't. The only thing you're missing is processed chemicals, cancer-causing chemicals, nutrient and vitamin-empty foods.

Does that really sound like something you should be missing?

You only have one body and one brain. Do you want to shovel shit into them like the cookie monster, or turn them into a work of art?

Your choice.

Ch. 5 - Women Should Put YOU on a Pedestal

Alright, now it's time for your favorite chapter.

By and large, when men think of an Alpha Male, they think of one thing: a guy who gets women. Sure, the idea of financial success, nice cars, vacation homes and all that is just dandy—but what really puts the alpha in Alpha Male is the ability to dominate.

And what says dominate more than having women at your beck and call?

Every guy wants it. A curvaceous babe, head between his legs as he sits with a stoagie in one hand and his other hand on her head, guiding the action. Every guy wants it. A beautiful, sensual woman, riding high and wild atop his manhood, as the room echoes with her cries and whimpers.

Every man wants a beautiful woman.

And if you know what to do, you can get her.

See, too many guys are intimidated. They see a woman and they ultimately think sex. They think about the woman naked, they think about how they're coming across, they think that the woman is going to instantly judge them, dismiss them, and find somebody better.

Well, with that attitude she will!

The trick to attracting beautiful women is to not care one bit that they're attractive. Think of it this way. Beautiful women everywhere are tired of guys wanting them. They're tired of guys who leer, stare, and drop their jaws with drool. They're tired of nervous guys and macho guys who approach with the same worn and wearied pick-up lines; guys who immediately think sex when they see women.

The Alpha Male is not thinking about sex when he sees a hot babe. In fact, the Alpha Male is thinking about everything *but* sex. When a beautiful woman walks into his field of vision, he barely acknowledges her. Instead of staring, or looking, or attempting to steal glances when she isn't looking, the Alpha Male will give one penetrating gaze—no more than 2 seconds—before looking away.

The reason the Alpha Male doesn't look at beautiful women is because they're used to it. He knows it and they know it. And he also knows something else. He realizes, unlike most men, that beautiful women are often the most insecure. Although this seems counter-intuitive, the truth is easily explained. Beautiful women have been told their entire lives how beautiful they are. So what do they do? Well, they set their bar high, expecting guys who are just as beautiful. In the long-term, these expectations are rarely met. As a result, the beautiful woman begins to doubt her beauty. So many guys assume that she will turn them down that they never even approach her, or they approach her with extreme nervousness. In either case, the beautiful woman begins to assume that she isn't what she thought. As her less attractive friends meet guys and end up happy, the beautiful woman ends up alone. Add intelligence into the mix, and a beautiful and smart woman may almost seem destined for loneliness.

This is where the Alpha Male comes in. He sees this insecurity and he finds the perfect balance. Instead of ignoring the woman altogether, he gives her small, fleeting bits of attention. He is not nervous when he does it; he is calm and casual. In the end, this is what wins over a beautiful women.

Of course, this is not to say that the Alpha Male targets insecure women. After all, there are plenty of floozies who will spread their thighs far and wide—there is nothing special about these women. What the Alpha Male pursues, however, *is* special. He goes after beautiful women because he knows, even if they're insecure, that he can bring them around. He can nurture, empower, and ultimately unlock the Alpha within a beautiful, intelligent woman. And once that inner strength is unleashed, the Alpha Male and the Alpha Female create a power couple unlike any other…

Of course, this all hinges on the Alpha Male's ability to seduce the beautiful woman. In order to do this, the Alpha Male is exceedingly perceptive. He knows how to move in social settings, how to navigate his way through throngs of scantily-clad, highly attractive females. He understands the science of sex. He understands the power of magnetism.

But more than anything, he understands how to talk to women.

When a beta male sees a hottie, he stares. This stare indicates that he considers her some kind of goddess. It also indicates that he is probably horny and not experienced with women.

So why would a woman ever find this attractive? The man is doing nothing but signaling that he appraises his own status below the female's.

This may occasionally work for lunatic, power-hungry chicks—but with most women, it will fail and fail miserably.

Women want men who are self-assured not men who are incapable of managing their basic desires. Females crave guys who value themselves so much so that they would never forsake their own beliefs and values—even for the hottest chick in the world.

When a man is confident with *or* without a woman, all women find this attractive. It means that the man can do his own thing. It means he doesn't validate himself through another. It means that he's unafraid to stand on his own two feet, on his own terms.

Men who are constantly pursuing women, who are in and out of relationships or flings, are men who are weak and needy. They need women because without a woman, they feel like failures.

Alpha Males, however, don't care. They'll get a woman when they want one, but they certainly don't *need* one.

This is why Alpha Males are so attractive to women. This is why they can give women the orgasmic sex that others cannot. Alpha Males will eventually find their queen, a woman of tremendous power and potential.

But like any queen, she must have a king. And it is the Alpha Male that fills this role.

In order to fit this role, a man must learn how to read women. Firstly, look good. Whatever you're wearing, look good. Have your own style, but make it a style that makes sense. It should be *cohesive*, it should come together from head to toe. But more than anything, it should be you. Wear a style that truly represents you. For most men, dressing up makes them feel confident. Their hair is combed, their cologne is on, their shirts and pants ironed and well-fitted. Whatever your style, make sure that you feel good about it. You don't want to feel fake or phony wearing something, just because somebody *else* told you it looks 'good on you.'

Once your clothing is right, make sure that you know how to talk to women. When approaching a woman, look once from afar, and one more time while walking toward her. Walk with purpose and walk direct, and don't stare as you walk. Acknowledge others as you approach your target.

Once near your target, hold eye contact and say something simple. This is where too many guys mess up. They think they have to sweep the woman off her feet with some ingenious pick-up line. This is false. In fact, research shows that simple questions are the best. Simple questions that reduce tension by drawing simple observations about the surroundings.

You might say something as easy and meaningless as, "Pretty crowded in here, isn't it?" or "How are you doing?" or "Pretty warm in here, huh?" The point is to lower her guard with a question that forces an easy response. It's a simple way to get a harmless conversation going. Being mindful of your setting allows you to make an observation that, while superficial, is totally non-threatening and sends the clear cue, 'I want to talk to you.'

Once you've done that, learn how to position yourself. Don't face her straight on, because you don't want to see totally invested, but don't totally face away from her either. Keep your body open with your arms resting on a chair or comfortably at your side and no objects between you and the lady. Occasionally look away in thought or when pausing between words. Make intermittent contact for no more than 3 seconds at a time. Feel free to keep your eyes roaming for other females and don't be afraid to smile or acknowledge them verbally—this will only turn up the heat and make the girl you're talking to want you even more

Basically, be yourself. Not all Alpha Males have to be serious and contemplative. You can be humorous, you can be self-deprecating, you can be curious and childish. The trick is to show that you can be a lot o things, that you're *versatile*.

Keep your voice mostly steady and your demeanor calm, but don't be afraid to throw in bursts of unexpected behavior to catch her off guard and keep her interested. Girls like guys that can show a little bit of emotion—a little bit of empathy, compassion, tenderness, or warm-heartedness.

Beta Males will stand stiff afraid to be themselves. Alpha Males will recognize the importance of showing their true colors, as long as those colors are never exposed for too long or too intensely. Remember, you are just getting to know this woman, there's no logic in showing her your whole hand. You want to tempt her, to lead her along, to keep her guessing about who you are and what you stand for. Women love men who have mysterious quality.

So tease her. If she asks you what you do, don't respond like most men and throw out some cheesy job title. Turn the question around on her, or pretend not to hear, or jokingly space out and pretend to have forgotten, or even be bold and say something like, "I'd tell you, but then I'd have to kill you."

The trick is to be unconventional. Now that the two of you have been talking for a little bit, there's nothing wrong in being different. In fact, it's what women want. And you'll know if they want *you*, as their body language progresses.

Be observant. Sexually attracted women will display an array of chemistry markers. Firstly, they'll laugh, showing their teeth and wrinkling their eyes. They'll flip or toss their hair, often allowing it to touch or graze you. They'll show their wrists, indicating that they're submissive and honest. They'll make their cleavage more visible, their butts more prominent, their lips more plump—pretty much all of their 'assets,' they'll accentuate. They'll also put on makeup right in front of you.

Women who are attracted tend to do other things as well, like 'stumbling' into guys, brushing their arms, legs, butts or breasts against guys in passing or when leaning in, and pretending to tidy a guy up by brushing lint or dust off his clothing. Sexually attracted women will also have softer, slower voices than when speaking to people to whom they aren't attracted. These sexually stimulated females may also have flushed skin, increased perspiration and an obvious increase in the size of their pupils.

So be observant! And send the right body language back. Be the Alpha be the male. Steady a woman if she trips or pretends to lose her balance Give fleeting touches to her shoulder or the small of her back when the two of you laugh. Give her playful taps or even light punches. And always, *always*, proceed with caution. You never know how any woman will take your advances, and it's best to go slow than fast.

Besides, other women will respect you even more if they hear good things. Remember, women chat! If you mistreat one of their friends, they might all just blacklist you. Sorry, no sexy time!

Ch. 6 – Create Your Fortune & Never Look Back!

By this point, I've taught you all I can.

We've gone over what it takes to be an alpha male. We've discussed at length why Alpha Males are superior and successful, why they command the attention and respect of others, why they can seduce women almost effortlessly at times, and why they generally enjoy a healthier, happier, more vibrant lifestyle than most others.

We've discussed the importance of keeping your body and mind in optimal shape, the importance of the right body language, and the science of attracting beautiful women.

So then what's left?

Well, truth be told, the only thing left to do is up to *you.*

It's time to find your purpose in this life on this Earth, and it's entirely up to you. Do you want to be a doctor? Do you want to be a surgeon or a psychiatrist or a renowned humanitarian physician? Do you want to be high-powered lawyer?

How about a teacher or professor? Or a leader? Do you want to command the minds of the masses, to make decisions that better societies for future generations to come?

Are you a man of vision, a man of so much potential that you've yet to unlock? Are you, or are you not? The answer lies within you, I can only take you so far. If you truly want something, you'll go after it. If you want to be wildly rich and successful, only you can make it happen. If you want to sleep with amazing women whenever you please, only you can do it.

So know your niche. Answer your calling and follow the voices. Follow the voice that beats from both head and heart, the only voice that will ever matter when all is said and done.

Don't succumb to your critics. Don't allow the broken dreams, lost passions, shattered hopes of others to bring you down. Understand that there will always be dissenters, naysayers. Realize that plenty of people will want to see you fail, because then that means that they are not alone. It means that they have somebody else to focus on, to withdraw from their own problems.

Do you want to be old and wrinkled, sitting in front of your T.V. yelling at the government, blaming politicians and leaders and random people you've never met for the failures of your life? Is that what you want?

Or do you want to be a winner? A man who had the freakin balls to grab life and say "Fuck it" and go full-head of steam in the direction of his dreams?

Are you a man that taps out after the first round, or do you keep going, keep taking a beating until you throw the perfect punch, make the perfect move, find the perfect strategy to finally claim the victory you've been seeking?

When you're old and fading, sitting on your deathbed and reviewing the many moments that made your life… what will you think?

Will you remember the things you did great, the days, moments and experiences that brought you success? Will you remember the life of an Alpha?

Or a life lost?

A Special Note:

Thank you for reading *"The Alpha Male: MAN UP and Unlock Your Alpha – An Overnight Guide to Conquering Fear, Women, and Lifelon* *Success"* If you enjoyed reading this book and would like to be included on an email list for when similar content is available, feel free

<u>SUBSCRIBE</u>

As always, thank you for reading. And may you continue to live healthily and happily.

Sincerely,

<u>C.K. Murray</u>

Other works by C.K. Murray:

1.   <u>*Mindfulness Explained: The Mindful Solution to Stress,*</u> <u>*Depression, and Chronic Unhappiness*</u>

2.   <u>*Emotional Intelligence Explained: How to Master Emotional*</u> <u>*Intelligence and Unlock Your True Ability*</u>

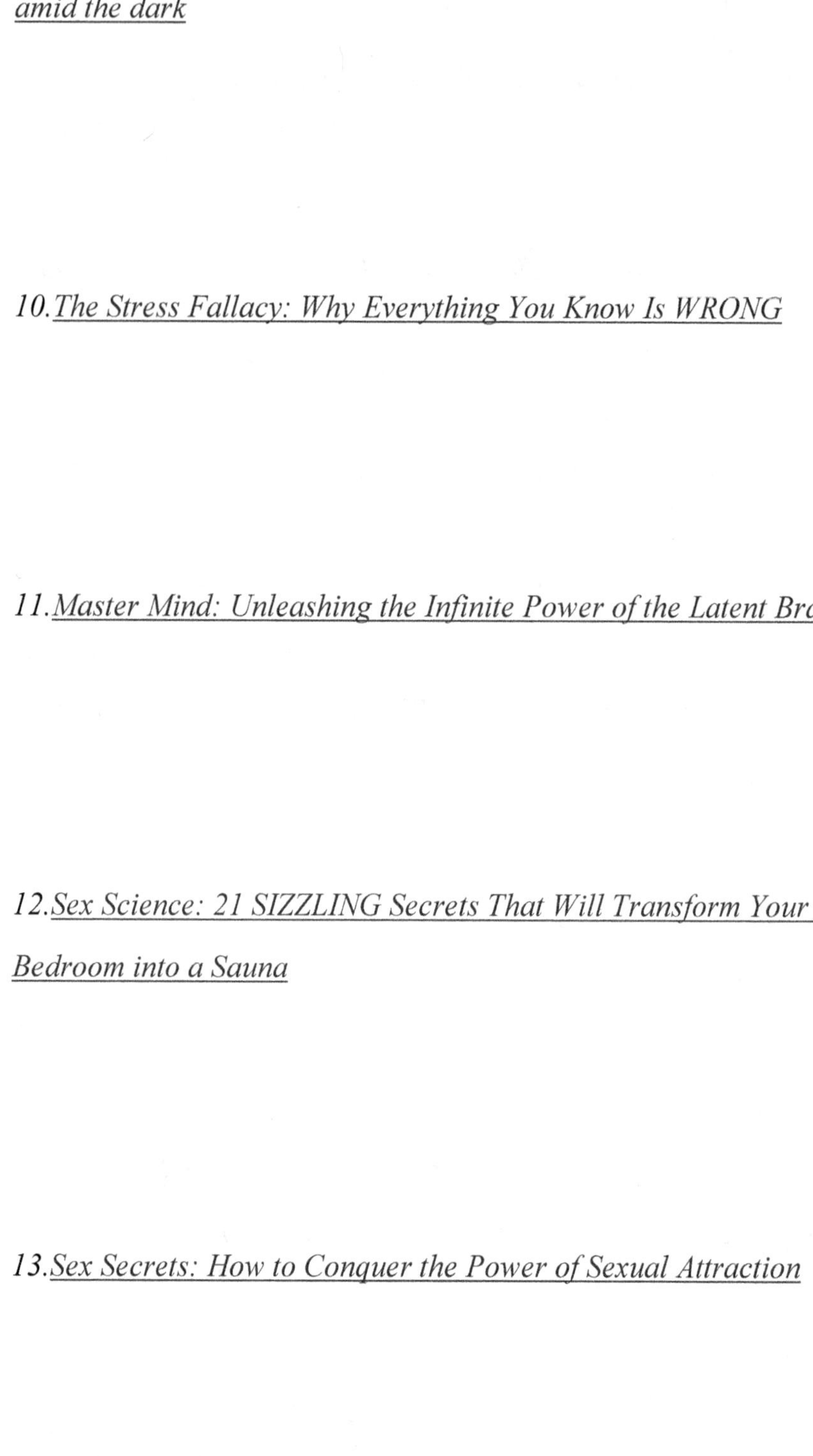

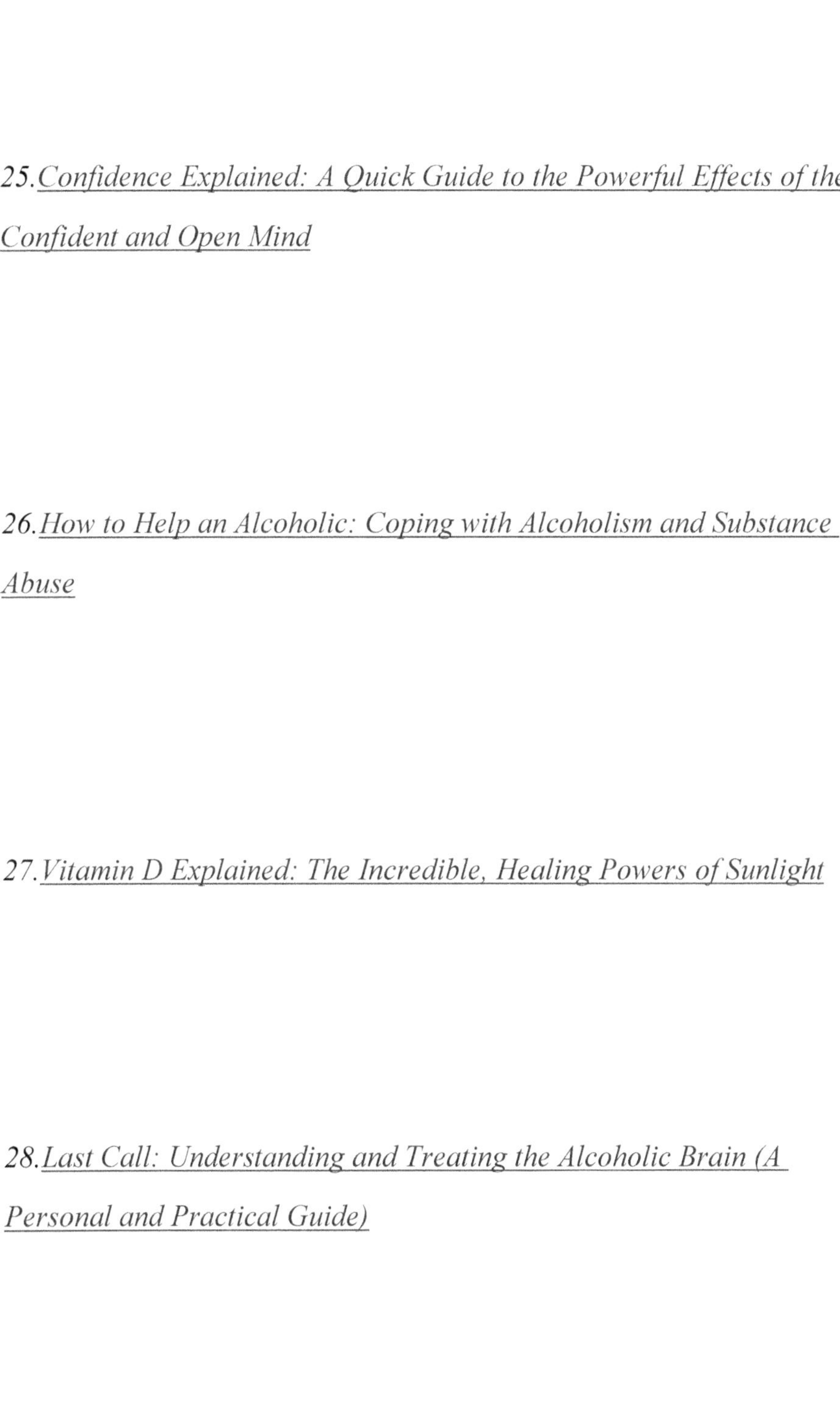

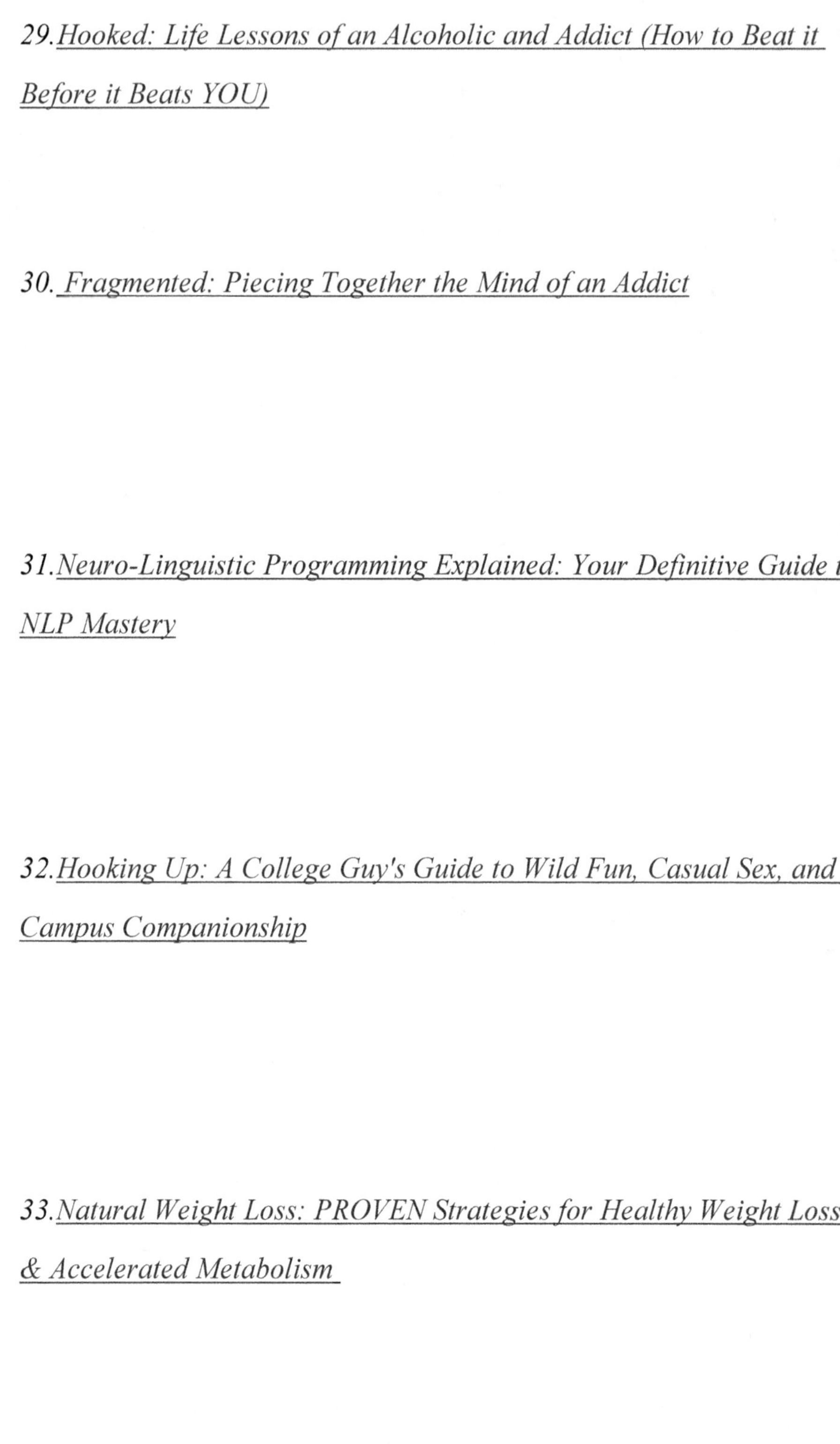

www.ingramcontent.com/pod-product-compliance
Lightning Source LLC
Chambersburg PA
CBHW051920250726
48659CB00002B/761